God on Earth

The Lord's Prayer for Our Time

God on Earth

Text by Will Campbell

Photographs by Will McBride

Poetry by Bonnie Campbell

Crossroad

1983

The Crossroad Publishing Company
575 Lexington Avenue
New York, New York 10022

Library of Congress Cataloging in Publication Data

Campbell, Will D.
  God on earth.

  1. Lord's prayer. I. Campbell, Bonnie. II.
Title.
BV230.C15 1983   242   82-23603
ISBN 0-8245-0550-6   0-8245-0586-7 pbk.

Our Father
who art in heaven
hallowed be thy name.
Thy kingdom come.
Thy will be done
on earth
as it is in heaven.
Give us this day our daily bread
and forgive us our trespasses
as we forgive those
who trespass against us.
Lead us not into temptation
but deliver us from evil.
For thine is the kingdom
and the power
and the glory
forever.
Amen.

Our Father

Our *Father.* אבא That's the way it would have looked if their friend and teacher had written it in his native Aramaic. And maybe he did. Squatting on the barren soil on a hillside in Galilee he might have scribbled the words in the dirt as he did at other great moments.

אבא, looking to us now like chicken scratchings. If he just said it aloud it sounded like "abba," some kind of baby talk to one's daddy. Or the way we talk to little babies when we are pretending they are talking to us. "Ya' itsie, bitsie, intsie baby, dad-die loves you." Abba. Abba. See ya' daddy.

If he wrote it in the sand, in a short while the wind blew it away forever.

Forever gone. From the bleak and fallow landscape of the Galilean ground they sat upon. Forever echoing and reverberating through the ages, the Pentecostal dust sifting and translating the symbols into every tongue. The genial winds of grace scattering and dropping each syllable upon every land as they blew. Gone forever everywhere. Abba. Daddy. Pop. Pater Noster. Vater Unser. Uren Fader.

Notre Père. Nostro Papa.

From a lonely roadside in Galilee to Nacogdoches, Texas. From Miletus to Hiroshima, Galatia to Baghdad, Pergamum to Lake Tahoe, Macedonia to Selma, Alabama. Pamphylia, Wake Island, Zurich and Warsaw. Sidon to Port Adelaide. Cappadocia, Nairobi, Hudson Bay and Pretoria. From Philippi to Earth's Moon. Patmos to Pasadena. The dust scattered. Places. Our *Father.*

And events. Coronation of queens at Westminster Abbey and revival meetings under an Appalachian brush arbor. Blessing of the shrimp fleet in Gulfport and last words uttered on the sinking Titanic. Matins at a convent school in Kenya and baccalaureate at Harvard. Blue and gray at Gettysburg. Christian killing Christian. Our Father. Ecclesia and aimless vagrants. A dying old man's baptism in a bathtub and a little girl's confirmation in San Juan. Our Father.

Teach us to pray. Strange that they would ask him that, this little band of vagabonds who had been a praying people since the days of Abraham. Like seasoned cowboys asking the trail boss to teach them how to ride a horse.

"Teach us to pray."

And he did. "Do it this way," he told them.

"When you pray say, 'Our Father.'" Dear Abba. The first tentative and informal sound made at the baby's first taste of wheat.

Father. KINFOLKS!

Not "Our *God*." Gods aren't kin to folks. "Our *Father*." No doubt they had heard God referred to as Father before, but not very often. Most often the image they heard the rabbis use was of King. Or Lord. The idea of sonship, of actual kinship had not been developed. Fathers are kinfolks! God is God and a human is a human. God has claims and designs on us but we have no claims and designs on God. God is God. But kinfolks have claims and designs on each other. Kinfolks ask each other for things: Give us some bread, something to eat. Don't hold things against us. Forgive us. Excuse and understand. Comfort and accept us. Protect and defend us. Keep us away from the Evil One. Keep the Evil One away from us.

Kinfolks is a good idea. But kinfolks kill one another too.

Dark-eyed, olive-skinned little thing snuggling in your beard. "Nice Father," she purrs. "Abba. Abba."

Wet baby, nestled against your bare skin, fourteen minutes out of his mammakin's body. But look out!

Our *Father*. "We'll kill you."

Say, "Abba. Pop. Pappa. Daddee," Jesus told them. They must have been confused at the time. God heretofore had been farther away than that. God is God and a human is a human. Now God and we are kinfolks. Certainly it would not have occurred to them that God could be executed by the government like an ordinary human being. They hadn't understood his mission. For God to be a human and be killed by human hands— cross, gallows, guillotine, electric chair, gas chamber, lethal injection—so that kinfolks and God might be reconciled. Children saved. Delivered. From sin and death, the last enemy. Brothers and sisters everyone.

Evermore.

For God's sake then. Don't blow up the world. You'll kill His kinfolks.

Who art in heaven

Far Far away. Father has gone on a long trip. Kinfolks generally stay close by. Across the river. Up the bayou. Down the street. In Brooklyn or Salinas. We fly out to see them in the summertime. Drive over on rainy Sunday afternoons. Walk next door to play catch with cousins. Open house every day at papa and mama's house. Thanksgiving dinner at grandma's. Family re-union at the old home place every fourth Sunday in May.

In heaven? A father in heaven? Kinfolks far away. Higher than up. Farther than distance. Sea above and sea below. Higher than eagles or astronauts fly. Farther than the sun. Farther than radar signals reach. Beyond Mars and Jupiter, the Milky Way and the North Star. So far. In heaven. Everywhere. Nowhere.

That must have bothered them. To hear that their new-found Father was in heaven. That's what Peter and Andrew had been told when their baby brother died. "He's gone to heaven." And James and John when their mother passed away. It was just before they quit fishing for a living and followed the stranger. "She's in heaven."

The first word of the prayer had made them happy. Abba. The first word of a weaned baby. Kinfolks. Then confusion and uncertainty again. God is where dead kinfolks go. Father in heaven.

But we'll find Him. We'll build a tower. Big pretty steeples. Do nice things to please Him. We'll lure Him back.

Babel. Babel. Babel.

Sound and fury. Satellite folly. Distant drums. One glimpse through a dark glass.

Elusive kin.

Not only far away but silent too. More than a million people saying those words every second of every minute. Each ticking of the clock somewhere on earth a million voices are saying it. And in two thousand years not once has the answer come back:

"Yes, my child."

Does He not care? Is He not there? Is He not kinfolks after all?

Say it anyway, Jesus said. Say, "Our Father in heaven." Say it in secret. Knock. Seek. Find. Hide and say it. Hide in a dark closet and talk to a Father hiding beyond the moon.

TRUST. The nonsense of TRUST.

Heaven comes close. Fallen

sparrows are marked. Hairs are numbered. The doors of prisons are opened. Dead are raised. Sick are healed. Lepers are clean. Deaf hear. Blind see. The poor hear good news.

The Father who is in heaven has come down to earth. And is in your midst.

Go tell it on a mountain!

Colonizers

We love exotic places,
love saying their names,
feeling them turn around
on the tongue
the way a face might turn
in recognition on the street
or a sound might become
a voice
convincing us that there
outside the window
someone is sweating.
The places we love lead us
outside our skin
often too far or far enough
that the cord between our love
and the place snaps
and graffiti turns up
in Selma, New Delhi,
and the jungles of Laos.

Hallowed be thy name

Father has a name. Of course. They had heard and used it many times. Abraham didn't have a name for God so he made one up. Yahweh.

But Jesus didn't use that name. His usage almost made it appear that the name for the Father he addressed was "Hallowed." It was a word of extremes, of peculiar opposites.

Look at that strange word: First, "hallo." It means, "Get 'um, dogs. Sic 'um." It was the sound of the hunter's urging from close behind the hounds. Then "halloo," the same imperative but now from a great distance, a cry from over the mountain or the other side of the forest. The object is far away and the pursuer screams in desperation. And finally "hallow," the worthless part of the rabbit thrown to the dogs as reward for their obedience and success.

But in this case *Hallowed*. A tense already accomplished but also continuing to be accomplished. Something they were to do because the Father had already done it for them. A sacred, near unmentionable and unapproachable designation. Let the name of the Father be hallowed. As a reward we toss Him a hallow. God is the dogs of the chase. He pursues, chases, catches, and lays it at our feet. We keep everything and fling him a hallow, something useless, unneeded. God doesn't need our prayers. God has no needs. *We* need the prayers. Hallowed be Thy name. Please.

Did you ever watch a young child struggle to tell you her mother's name? "What's your mamma's name, child?"

"Mamma."

"I mean, I know she's your mother. But what's her real name?" At first the child is confused. Her name is just "Mamma." And even when she understands it is difficult for her to say, "My mamma's name is Brenda." The phonetic sounds of "mam-ma" have a protective ring, a cuddling closeness. "Brenda" sounds impersonal and removed. Even harsh for the tender ears of a two-year-old taught to call out for "Mamma." The disciples must have felt that as Jesus taught them to pray. The child, in her childishness, doesn't need another word for Mamma. Or for Daddy. She doesn't need to be told that they are good, dependable, protective. She knows all that. She doesn't have to be taught to hold them close, to cry out to them when she is hurt, wet or hungry, to crawl and reach out to them when a stranger comes too close. That's instinct. Years later she might spend hours on the analyst's couch trying to reconstruct the relationship, or trying to figure out where it went awry. But the infant has no such concern.

Jesus was moving them beyond the infant stage in bringing them to a proper understanding of God through a life of prayer. They wondered why he spent so much time in prayer. Perhaps that was why they asked him to teach them. He spent time in prayer because he had the proper relationship. He simply enjoyed fellowship with the Father. Visiting with kinfolks. When they asked him to teach them how to visit with kinfolks he brought them step by step through the process.

First, the childish stage, the baby talk. "Say, 'Abba. Abba.'" It is the infant in the nursery stage when the breast of the mother is no more than a whimper away. And now the father offering a feeding of porridge.

We cannot be sure of the timing here. It might have been days or weeks before he gave them the second lesson in the ideal and appropriate prayer. Maybe they had reveled in those first two words for a long time, happy that they had asked him to tell them how he prayed. They understood the analogy and it was easy. Praying is like saying, "Hi, Dad." Maybe much later he said, "But be careful. It isn't like going fishing with the old man. When you say, 'Hi, Dad' be sure you add 'in heaven' because Father is: Higher than eagles fly. Further than the compass points."

Still later the third instruction. One which would banish the seeming anthropomorphous notion of "Our Father" to the realm of awe: "Hallowed be Thy name." The baby talk is gone now. Father's name stretches to the other side of the forest and over the mountain and farther still. Hallowed! Separation. But not estrangement. Remoteness. But not alienation. The name of the Father was so sacred their ancestors would not utter the sounds.

God is God is God is God is God is God and then a period.

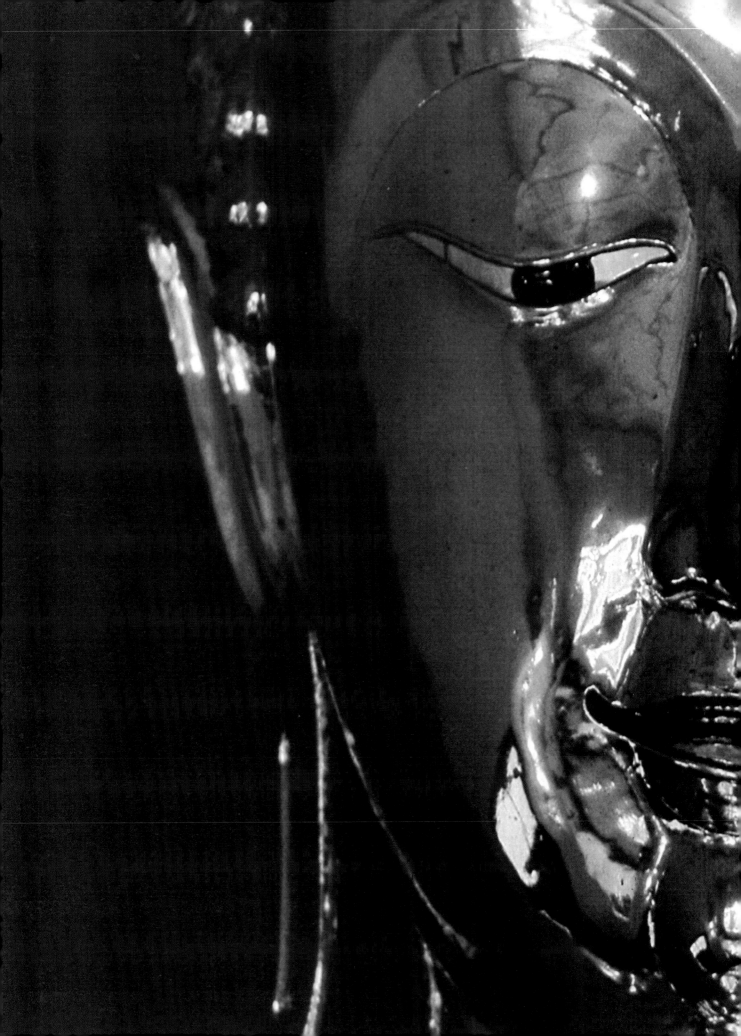

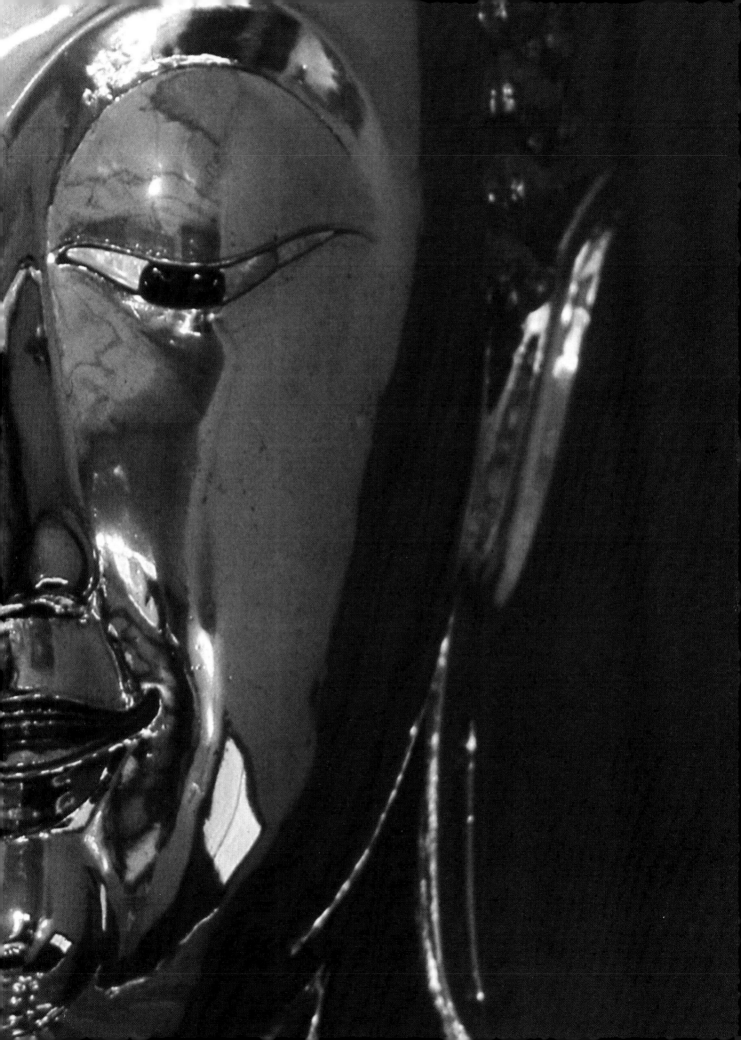

Our Father, who art in heaven, Hallowed be Thy name. With just ten words Jesus had given them a theology, the only theology possible. A theology of the absolute sovereignty of God. And even "absolute sovereignty" are insufficient words for the wordless One. Two thousand years, thousands more books, and millions upon millions of words later the theology survives, and is all we can affirm about the Father with categorical certainty: God is God is God is God is God is God and then a period.

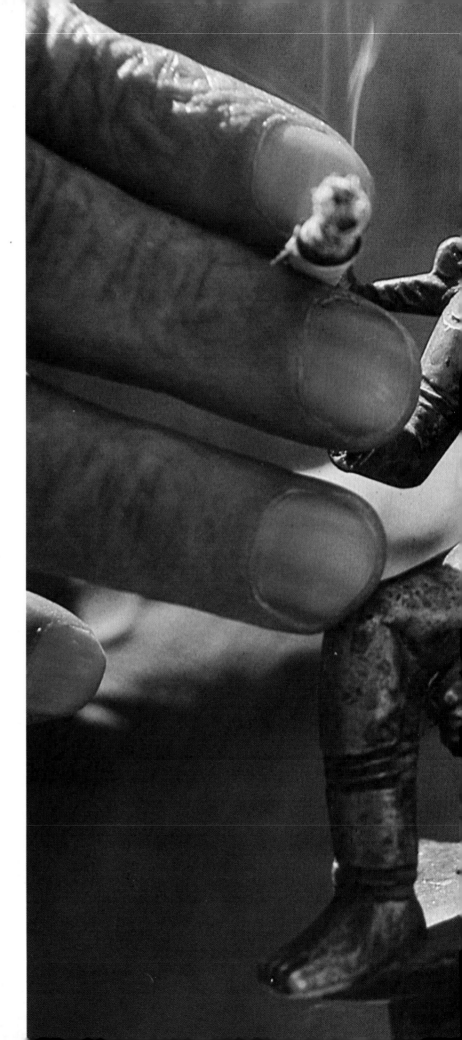

Thy kingdom come

Sometimes we confuse the things we wish *for* with the things we hope *in*. We *wish* for a world in which there would be no crime, no war, no disease, no wanton destruction of the forests nor poisoning of the streams, no discrimination on the basis of race, gender, or religion. To say that this has not come true is a gross understatement. Our *hope* is in the Lord. And then in a kingdom, His kingdom. Our frail assumption is that it is a kingdom in which the things wished for would be taken for granted. We are bold to ask that the two become one. We ask the Father to bring His reign to earth. Thy kingdom come.

Are we serious? Or do we pray the prayer assuming that the kingdom of God would be pretty much like the kingdom of Caesar? Maybe a few more sacred art pieces to adorn the walls and cute little cherubs picking flowers all day while some empyrean Muzak beams Handel's oratorios from above. But otherwise not much change.

Not so. The prayer has become tough now. Earlier it had been gentle and comforting. Baby talk to a caring sire, followed by a sort of cheering section: May your name be holy! May your name be holy! Yea, Abba! Abruptly Jesus begins to tell them what it is appropriate to ask for. And the very first petition is so outrageous. So far beyond the limits of what we honestly want because it would totally change the world we live in.

Since we are not the Father, we can but speculate as to what His kingdom would be. But from what we learned of Him from the person of Jesus we can make certain assumptions.

Because the morality of God is perfection we would assume that His kingdom would be one without crime. But if crime were removed from the present era the economy would collapse. Our brother/son, Webb Campbell, is a student of law. In a reign without crime he would have to change his professional direction. No crime, no lawyers. Licenses for marrying, driving, hunting, and the regulation of commerce would not be necessary, so courthouses would be useless except for keeping the census. And what would be the point of that? Sell the courthouses and give the money to the poor. If none breaks the law there is no need for legislatures to pass and repeal laws. And no judges, sheriffs, J.P.s, bail-bond companies, prison guards, wardens, warrant servers, court clerks or bailiffs. No contractors to build jails and no staff to run them. Police departments, highway patrolmen, the F.B.I. and private investigators would be unemployed. And what need for a president, vice-president, 100 senators and 435 congressmen and their staffs? Let them go to work in something useful. (Wonder how often the Senate chaplain says the Lord's Prayer on the Senate floor.) Guess all of us had better be careful how we pray for a kingdom without crime.

Pray: Thy kingdom come.

A kingdom without war? Do we want it? More than half the economy is somehow related to it. No Pentagon? Army, navy, marine corps, and their academies? No fifty billion dollars for weapons this year? No munitions manufacturers, barracks builders, vending machines for the troops? Not even bus drivers to take anti-nuclear demonstrators to New York or hotels to house them and restaurants to feed

them. No United Nations on Manhattan Island. How many millions of people are making their living in war-related industries? What would we do with them?

Better be careful how we pray for a reign without war. Yet Jesus said, "Pray, Thy kingdom come."

A kingdom without disease? No doctors, nurses, medical schools, hospital administrators and orderlies. No health insurance policies, drug manufacturers, pharmacists, paramedics or Hospital Corporation of America.

When you pray, say: Thy kingdom come.

A kingdom with air birds could fly in, and streams fish could swim in and boy scouts could stoop and drink from on their hikes. But where would we pour the acrid smoke and foul leavings, the residue of our indulgences? Perchance no clamoring for the indulgences?

Thy kingdom come?

St. Paul talked about the kingdom. Neither male nor female. Black nor white. Educated nor ignorant. No discrimination. And what would that cost?

What if we pray the prayer

23

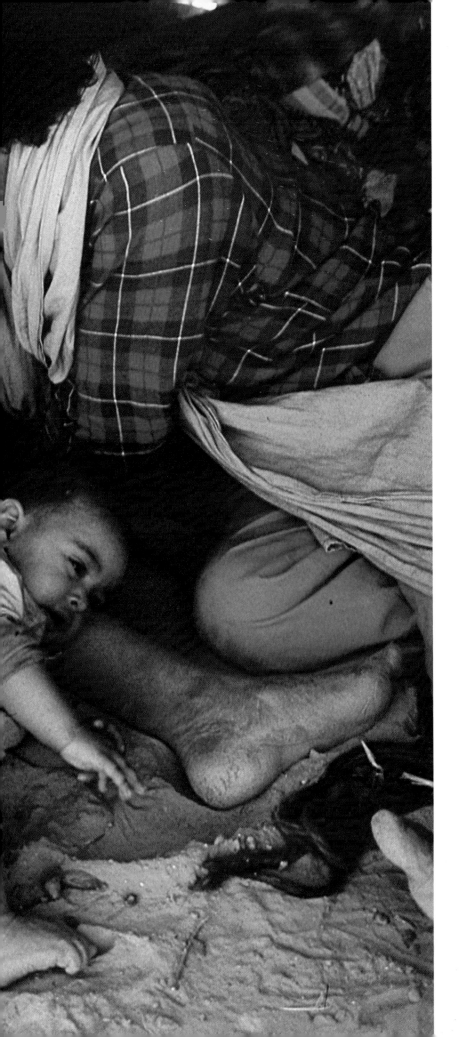

just one time too many and it is answered?

It is already answered. The advent of a utopian society is not the only way to view these words of Jesus. Another approach is that the kingdom is already here, has been ushered in by the Son of the Father, Jesus himself. And the call to the kinfolks of God is for our participation in it. Just live what already is. That which *is* has been revealed by this Son of the Father. Our joint heir.

The kingdom of which he spoke is locked in relentless combat with the kingdom of this world, the kingdom of evil. We are praying that the kingdom of the Father will win. Which it already has. We are choosing between the two, offering our services in this ministry of reconciliation.

We *wish*. We also *hope*. Our *wish* is for the things we desire. Our *hope* is in the Lord. Who made heaven. And also earth. The prayer Jesus taught us is that the kingdom is for us.

Thy kingdom come.

Thy will be done

Have thine own way, Lord.
Have thine own way.
Thou art the potter,
I am the clay.

We sang the old hymn at home and on Sundays at the church house. It is a prayer. Hold o'er my being absolute sway! Power —all power—surely is thine! It was a dangerous prayer we sang. As radical as the one Jesus told the seekers to recite. Thy will be done. Really?

Joe, brother/uncle, when he was a yearling boy, used to dig heavy clay from ditches and road banks, sculpt it into busts of Washington or Lincoln and bake them in the sun of Mississippi dog days until they were as hard as the rocks that dotted the hillsides. Occasionally an air bubble, too much sand in the mud or an excess of moisture would cause the forms he shaped to crumble into tiny pieces. When such imperfections resulted in failure he would start again, knowing that not even his skilled hands could force their will upon the intractable earth. He had no other choice.

The farmer's plow, whether pulled by sturdy oxen or giant diesel machines, must deal with a force and will beyond its own. Despite his best effort, determination, expertise, the richness of the land and the quality of the seed, fruition relies finally upon the will of the elements.

A lone figure plays in the floodtide sands, secure in the mild waves that frolic about his toes, yet frightened by the knowledge that the thousands of miles of water now gently nudging the ripples can in an instant flex their pelagic muscles and pound the piers and beachhouses to splinters.

Thy will be done.

To court the will of the Father is to risk the abandonment of our own, the total submission of our will to His. Jesus, facing imminent execution, stated his own preference in the matter but immediately added: ". . . nevertheless, not my will, but as Thou wilt." Praying that the will of God be done takes us back to the lunacy of placing our mind, soul, body and all our worldly goods in a blind trust. It was not an easy prayer for Jesus but it was an honest one. For us it is quite easy and we do it all the time. When we find it to be easy

we can know that in all likelihood we don't really mean the words we are mouthing.

When stripped of wealth, health, happiness, friends and family, despite a long life filled with righteousness, Job refused to give up either the God he trusted or the righteous life. To those who sought to dissuade him he said, "Hold your peace, let me alone. . . . Though He slay me yet will I trust in Him."

With our values, our notions of the way things ought to be for us, the will of God may be a bitter potion. The bottom line, what the petition is really about, is yet again God is God is God is God is God and then a period.

On earth

Earth, as a word, is about as vast, mysterious and incomprehensible as heaven. Both are introduced in the first verse of the Bible. "In the beginning God created the heaven and the earth." It was His creation. Then it was His gift to us as the land of our habitation. We are told it was a good land, a land of flowers, trees and pure water. Gold, onyx stone and sweet smelling bdellium were mentioned by the writer of Genesis. A big bright light to warm and rule the day. A soft, pleasant one to preside over the night. Stars to twinkle and flirt with the creatures below.

For reasons of His own God immediately turned what He had created over to us. "Here it is. I made it for you. It's a present." There must have been a rough wilderness quality about it too. "Subdue it" were the words he used. "Have dominion over it." And from the beginning we confused dominion with destruction. Like a child who responds to a new windup toy with a hammer to see what makes it run we approached the gift of earth with baneful purpose. Black hills upholstered with thick woods became the cutover corpse of greed, bringing in its wake erosion, dust storms and grapes of wrath. The gold of Havilah became the standard of commerce and usury and the mockery of God in flamboyant religious structures. The fragrance of bdellium gave way to the smells of mills and forges, all in the name of building a better earth for all people. Geography appeared, dividing the earth into kingdoms, dynasties, states and nations with the attendant violence to draw and defend the lines.

Almost from the beginning those who received the earth as a gift of the Father sought to appropriate the Kingdom of Heaven as well. "Let us build us a city and a tower, whose top may reach unto heaven. . . ." The towers have varied. From the primitive notion that the crude structure of stone and slime would serve as a vehicle to outwit the Father, to the conceit and arrogance of the academy as we seek to deliver ourselves with much learning. The result has been little more than a pattern of our own quilted ignorance. Our trees of knowledge have failed us time and again.

Why doesn't the Father put a

stop to it? If He truly loves us and if He is really all-powerful and all-knowing then why doesn't He simply stand between His children and keep them from killing each other? We have a young friend who was once given a beautiful acoustical guitar by his brother. After he had enjoyed it for two years he was about to trade it in for a stand-up amplifier to go with an electrical guitar he has acquired on his own. "But how can you do that, Bobby?" we inquired. "It was a present from your brother." "That's why I can do it," he replied. "It was not a loan. It was a present."

The earth was not a loan, it was a present. The Genesis account does not have God saying, "Here's the earth. I'm giving it to you, but if you don't take good care of it I'll take it back and run it right." Instead He said He was giving us complete dominion over it. In that act He gave us the same freedom He claimed for Himself.

The towers we build continue to be as destructive as He was creative, even to the point of total demolition of the earth in our efforts to become as God. God does seem to claim certain things for Himself, a prerogative He has not shared with us. He is God. But He does not run the earth. When Jesus was tempted with material wealth and political power if he would worship the Devil he did not say to the tempter, "But those things belong to God. They are not yours to give." The inference was that in fact they did not belong to God and His kingdom, but to an opposing power. God had given them away as surely as Michael had given Bobby the guitar. Can we not all remember how as children we would take our physical fights to the feet of a parent, wanting the parent to stop it? The wise one never did.

Despite all that, Jesus is praying, and teaching us to pray, that the same will that reigns in heaven may also reign on earth. "Thy will be done on earth. . . ." Was he instructing us to try to get the Father to change His mind after all? Even the affirmation of the Psalmist that "the earth is the Lord's and everything that is in it," might have been a cop-out, a sort of hint to the Lord to take back what He has given us and run it the way it should be run, to straighten out the mess we have made of

our inheritance.

Because the ways of God are so strange the answer to the petition may even now be coming and we are failing to recognize it. The *will* of *God* is a redundancy. The *will* of God cannot be repealed. The *wishes* of God, however, can be resisted in our freedom. But even the wishes of God may be coming through our very recalcitrance. Even as we fight to control the environment, and in the process deplete the natural resources, we may bring the towers crumbling around us. We shudder, for example, to think of a world without oil for energy. The brightest among us say that it will happen. In terms of the survival of the planet, what a happy issue would come out of such an affliction! If we had no energy we couldn't hurl nuclear missiles at each other across the globe. Bringing the wish, and will, of God to earth may mean turning the thermostat up, not down. Turning lights on, not off. Waste the energy for survival. Strange. Mysterious ways. In the wanton exercise of the freedom He gave us we may be bringing His will, and wish, to earth. And so we pray:

Thy will be done. On earth . . .

As it is in heaven

We know how it is on earth. It is little warm puppies and the slaughter of seven million Jews. It is Mother Teresa bathing the faces of the dying in Calcutta, and the outrage of Vietnam. It is a little girl trying to extinguish three candles on a birthday cake and succeeding, and a hundred thousand people trying to survive a lightweight bomb in Hiroshima and failing. It is what we call life and it is what we call death.

In heaven as on earth. We pray for the two to be as one. On earth we sometimes kill our babies before they cry and sometimes endure great sacrifice to nourish the weakest until their life's end. We elect mass killers to high office and strap one-time offenders in a chair and burn them to death with electric current. We applaud the cub scout who helps the elderly cross the street and cut aid to dependent children for the sake of still greater arms supplies.

Father. God. Yahweh. Adonai. Big Daddy. We're sick. We're all mixed up. We are sometimes up, and sometimes down. We are known to do noble deeds and we are known to do the most per-vasive and destructive evil.

Our Father, who art in heaven, we need help. Deliverance. Salvation. Thy will be done on earth the way it is done in heaven. Thy good be done on earth as Thy good is done in heaven.

The startling news about this petition was that it was answered in the person and presence of the teacher. It was not some kingdom, some will that would come in another thousand years if we prayed ardently enough. And if we worked, functioned, performed, produced sufficiently, or struggled gamely against the Evil One. Thy kingdom come, Thy will be done on earth as it is in heaven is a present reality— the reality of Christ. The kingdom had come to earth in the person of Christ. The will had been done on earth as in heaven in the person of Christ. God is in heaven. God is on earth. The kingdom is here. The will is here. Kingdoms of this world and their rulers come and go. The empire upon which the sun never set is now a tiny island. The Reich that would last a thousand years barely made a decade. The Roman Empire is no more. Hitler is dead and rotten. Stalin

is blotted from the history he wrote. America sits in the door of her cave, holding in her hand a suicidal and holocaustic grenade with pin pulled, glowering across the pond at an equally scared and similarly misguided neighbor.

The kingdom and will that came to earth in the person of Christ will prevail as certainly as at Golgotha. The kingdom, the reality of that Christ, is on earth as in heaven. We are not asked to build or to bring in that kingdom. Only to abide in it. But we are not forced.

Behold, he is coming with the clouds, and every eye will see him, every one who pierced him; and all the tribes of the earth will wail on account of him. EVEN SO. AMEN.

Give us this day our daily bread

*O Lord, won't you buy me a
 Mercedes-Benz.*
My friends all drive Porsches,
I must make amends.

"Bread."
"Well, what about honeybuns?"
"Bread."
"Hostess Twinkies? That's kind of like bread. And good too. Give us this day some fresh Hostess Twinkies."
"Bread."
"Popovers with strawberry jam inside are nice. Give us popovers: One cup milk. One cup flour. Two eggs. Half teaspoon salt. Bake at 525 degrees. Easy enough.
"And some vanilla wafers. We'll get some bananas at the A & P store and with what you furnish and what we get on our own we'll have a scrumptious banana pudding. Now how about it, Big Daddy, Abba, Father, God! We aren't asking for toasted English muffins, two scrambled eggs with Canadian bacon and half a grapefruit. (We have a serrated spoon though.)"
When you pray say, "Give us this day our daily bread."
"Well, could it be light brown, made of whole-grain rye, red spring wheat and golden flax seed? That's the healthiest kind, you know. They advertise it on television. And we'll buy some alfalfa sprouts at the health food store. Our body is your temple, you know."
"It may be tortillas."

When Jesus told his followers to pray for bread, for sustenance, he spoke as if the prayer would be answered. It is.
Why then do millions of people have no bread on this very day? Ten thousand of them will die of starvation by the time this day is over. At this very instant somewhere near or far a tiny baby whimpers her last as she sucks the cold and desiccated tit of a mother dead since yesterday. Why say the prayer for bread is answered? The mother died with the prayer of Jesus on her lips. At this moment somewhere near or far, as we pay lots of money to slenderizing salons to rid our bodies of the aftermath of our gluttony, a village is reeking with the smells of death and the sounds of the dying, squabbling for a cup of rice.

A father and mother wrestle

with the most momentous of all ethical decisons: Whether to eat the small loaf they have come upon or return to the refugee camp with it and run the risk of neither they nor their children being the ones who will get it.

What are we to make of this? Did Jesus lie when he told his disciples repeatedly that their requests would be granted? Before we make that judgment we had best read the prayer again, looking especially at the pronouns. Nowhere are the pronouns "I," "me," or "my" used. Only "our." And "us." It is not "my father" but "our father." The prayer for bread is not a singular or individual one. It is not, "Give *me*," but "give *us*." Years ago some of us were doing a survey in a large American city. In one apartment we found two little boys seated at the kitchen table. One of them was eating something we didn't recognize from a small bowl. After visiting a few minutes we asked him why his brother was not eating. "Cause he ate yesterday," he replied. "Yeah. I ate yesterday," the other one said. There was sad resignation in his voice but no resentment toward his brother.

The prayer is answered. There is bread abroad. There was nothing nationalistic about it. Jesus did not say, "Give those of us in Galilee daily bread." It was an all inclusive "us." Galileans and Texans. Israelis and Palestinians. Russians and Americans.

"Our father, . . . Give *us* bread for this day." The plea is heard. There is bread for all the Father's children. A drought in Asia but a bounteous harvest in Kansas. The scorching winds of summer blow across the Midwestern plains, leaving fodder in its wake while the alluvial deltas of the southland blossom from the same warm breath. The provided bread becomes missiles and submarines. Gifts of nourishment are diverted into agents of carnage. The bread is provided. The division is of our own doing. At our peril we turn the answered petition into political gambits.

Or we become fearful and obsessed with longevity. This day is not a very long time. The winter is coming and the forecast is gloomy. "Our father, . . . Give us this *year* our *yearly*-bread." The response comes back: "Take no thought for the morrow; for the morrow shall take thought for the things of itself." It was the prayer of an agitator. A harsh, radical statement of commitment of a Son to His Father. We *wish* for longtime security. We *hope* in the Lord of this day.

Our Daily Bread

In late July the honeysuckle
seduces the nose;
the tongue sucks sap
but hands never can collect
enough to fill a jar.
By mid-August the dry vines
smell like any other.
Not even the bees, those sugar pigs,
go near.
Like the moon when the honey's gone,
they're nothing special.
No old voice calls out,
"Suckle me honey."
The sap swells
and it's eaten.

And forgive us our trespasses

During the Great Depression a man, woman and five children moved wearily along a country road in the springtime and stopped at a farmer's house. They had walked across Oklahoma, Arkansas, and Louisiana. They had no food, no money and only the clothes they were wearing and the few things they could carry.

"We know how to work the land," they told a Mississippi farmer, "but we have no land to work. We lost all that we owned."

"I will let you use a share of my land," the man replied.

"We have no shelter."

"See that creek? If you follow it to the back side of the clearing you will find a small house."

"We will need furniture."

"There are beds there. A table and chairs and a few other pieces. Use them as if they were your own."

"We have no team. No tools to plow and cultivate the fields. No fertilizer. Not even seeds for planting."

"All that will be provided," the farmer told them. "I will buy you clothes and shoes and straw hats to shield you from the sun.
And food enough to get you through the season."

Throughout the summer their needs were met, and when autumn came and it was time for the land to rest the harvest was bountiful. There was cotton to sell, corn for bread, dried fruits and beans for winter.

They came again to the farmer's house. "We are moving on," they said. "Before we go we have come to ask if we owe you anything."

"You owe me everything," the farmer said. "The land, seeds, food, teams and tools. I owned it all. You brought nothing with you and you lived well at my expense. Everything you have now you owe to me."

The dispirited sharecroppers turned to walk away. "But wait," the owner called. "You were strangers from a distant land and I took you in. I love you now. All of you. All that you have is yours to keep. I forgive the debt. You are free to go if you like. But you are also free to stay."

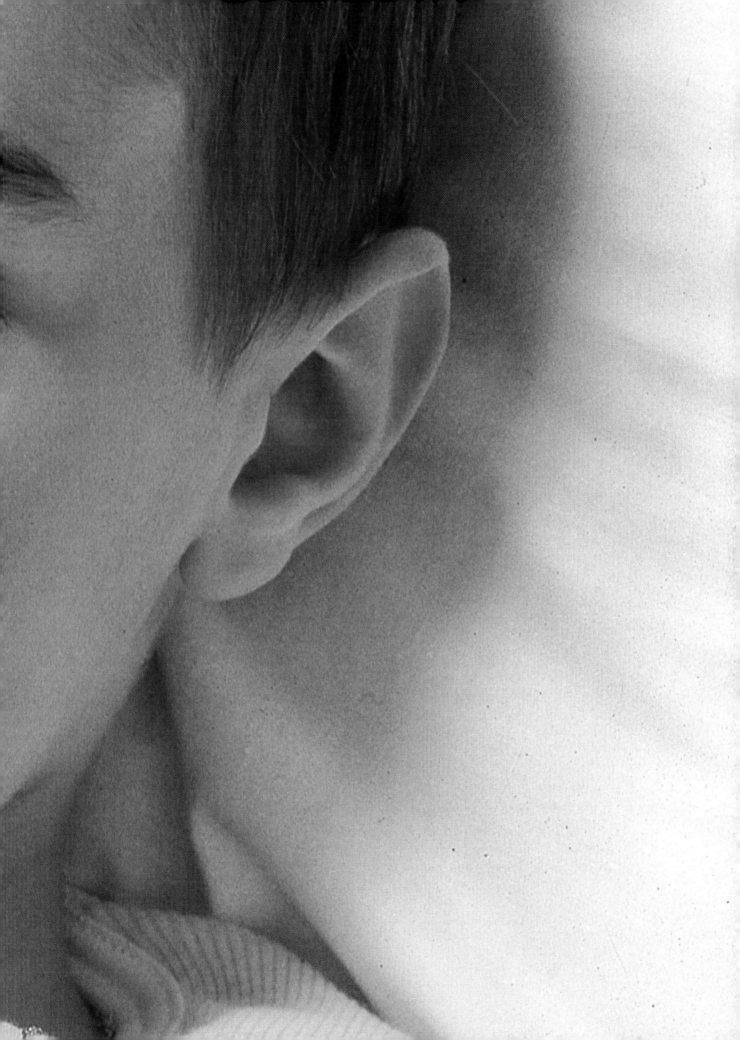

As we forgive those who trespass against us

> *You gave me my freedom,*
> *To go my own way.*
> *But you gave me much more;*
> *You gave me the freedom to stay.*

These are the words of a country love song Waylon Jennings sings. But they are equally expressive of the grace of God.

Grace that turns us loose: unearned, unmerited favors. Something done for us though we had no claim on it whatsoever. A gift with no strings attached. With it comes freedom. To squander the gift, to abuse it, deny its source, flaunt it as something earned. With it also comes freedom to abide in it, enjoy, cherish, adore and even to share it as an expression of thanksgiving to the donor. The freedom of grace is the story of the prodigal son and his elder brother. One chose a life of riotous living. The other chose to remain. The father understood.

> *You gave me my freedom,*
> *To go my own way.*
> *But you gave me much more;*
> *You gave me the freedom to stay.*

No one would deny that we have a debt to something or someone outside ourselves. Three minutes without air and we are dead. "Ah," we say, "but we know how to make air. We can take seventy-eight parts of nitrogen to twenty-one parts of oxygen, combine them with small amounts of argon, carbon dioxide, neon, helium and a few other gases and make our own air." The problem with that is that we are speaking of component parts to which we have given names but did not create.

We are debtors to God. When we pray that He will forgive us the debt, the trespass, we are quite literally asking that He overlook our "faults." We have defaulted on the mortgage. We are in His debt for everything because we are His creation. And even if we wanted to make it all up to Him, we're not even sure of His name. "Say that 'I AM THAT I AM' hath sent you," He said to Moses. God. Gott. Dio. Bokh. Mungu. Whatever name we choose we are left with mystery, wonderment and awe. Perhaps Jesus was speaking with reverent and befitting humor when he told his disciples just to call Him "Abba." Big Daddy. And ask the Big Daddy not to hold your faults against you.

The more we know the prayer is answered, the more we believe, the longer we are "Christian," the more convinced we are that we can never cease being in default. The more we are convinced that the sovereign Father —in heaven, with a hallowed name, the kingdom His, His will done, who provides us with sustenance, defends us at the time of trial—is, in fact, the one to whom we pray, the more frightening, intimidating, even terrifying the prayer becomes. No wonder the prayerbook prefaces this prayer in Holy Communion with the words: ". . . we are bold to say. . . ." Bold is a weak word for the presumption.

Forgive us our debts as we forgive the debts of others. What if we don't forgive our debtors, our trespassers, the faults of those about us? Does it mean that the faults which were overlooked previously will now become faults again and will not be forgiven? Not at all.

The Oklahoma family prospered with the generous overlord. Each year the land yielded good harvest and each year it was theirs to keep. One winter they bought the old Sabine family place across the river. It was rich bottom land with teams of strong young mules and many cattle. They hired illiterate hands to plant, cultivate and harvest the fields, and tend the herds. They charged them exhorbitant interest on the provisions they supplied, placed secret weights on the scales to deceive them and left them poorer at year's end than they were at the beginning. What will the farmer who forgave their debt do? Will he say, "I forgave what you owed me but now you have shown that you did not deserve it so it is back on my ledger?" If so, it is not grace after all. It is salvation by works. But that is not what the first farmer does. The debt of the Oklahoma vagabonds is wiped out forever. No matter what they do.

"As we forgive those who trespass against us" is not a proviso of an agreement. God does not play "you scratch my back and I'll scratch yours" with us. "As we forgive those who have offended us" is a two-sided touchstone. On the one hand I am able to forgive when the scary truth that I have been forgiven breaks through to me in all its

radical dimensions. On the other hand I can know that I am forgiven because otherwise I would not be capable of forgiving those who have defaulted in their debts to me.

The Oklahoma family saved a part of their earnings each year against the day their benefactor would come and demand that they repay him. When they were convinced that he would never do so they gave the money to the cheated laborers, divided the land and cattle with them and became their neighbors.

Under the Steel Light

I am being put to sleep,
laid out on a table
like a stumbling horse
or a woman in labor choosing not to see
the storm of birth.
I stare at the steel light
above the doctor's eyes and mask;
it explains my body better than a candle:
    The child navigates my belly
    suddenly turned storming.
I wake calling to the steel light calling:
    Give me back my blood
    my child
    my kin.

Under the steel light my tonsils throb.
The nuns cut paper dolls and count to
    ten slowly,
careful I don't see knife or needle . . .

    I slip off to school
    naked
    greeted with shrieks,
    hushed away to the sick room
    for surely I must be.
    I lie on a thin cot,
    my vain little body
    odd under tubes of light
    blinking,
    dreaming my thin legs are dancing.

I wake calling to the steel light calling:
    When I grow up will I have blood
        and breasts?

I imagine myself dead or dying,
running for my life
or curled in the crook of someone's arm.
I watch my hand turn out the light
and dream my legs are dancing down
    the hall.

Kingdom

At the pool there's a boy as dark
and round as a groundhog.
He waddles from shower to cement,
the water bully
eating a bag of Ruffles.
He suspects any moment
of holding something wonderful.
He pushes the smaller kids squealing—
silver knives slice the pool
throwing slivers of cold on my body
lying at high noon in the sun
thinking thickly of lunch, dinner,
sleep; vaguely cutting this day

from the day before
while the kids
circle the diving board
where the Groundhog holds forth
on the wonders of
*   head-first jumping.*
Like fat mantises
their arms arch in front of them
wild to hit the water
from the high board
in the sheer need to leap
beyond their skins.

The Beat Cat

This is a beat cat,
been to L.A. and back
on a coal car,

Listens to the sad jazz
of things
with one good ear.

Out in the real alley
where words hover and undress
the beat cat walks a tightrope

with no avenue audience—

he has upset someone's
idea of grace;
the word grace
takes off its clothes
in front of a mirror.

The beat cat
stays longer than usual
without laughing.

Lead us not into temptation

Don't take us too close to the ocean when the storm is coming, Father. You know we like to splash in the waves and we may be swept out to sea.

When you take us to the carnival we shouldn't walk too close to the frozen-custard stand. It makes us fat and rots our teeth.

Please don't let them build the cathedrals too tall. Our spines tingle at the sight of St. Ambrose in stained glass. We gasp with exhilaration at the sounds of the crescendo pouring from the giant pipes, massaging the ribs of the ogive, shaking the pinnacles above. It is all so overwhelming, so very, very beautiful. We might build a tabernacle on that mountain and never go down to the valley where your children are suffering and dying. So . . .

Lead us not into the temptation of worshipping the work of our hands, or worshipping worship, of making an idol of pleasant ritual.

Lead us not into the temptation of confusing the kingdoms of this world with Thy kingdom.

O beautiful for spacious skies,
For amber waves of grain,
For purple mountain majesties
Above the fruited plain!

We are already prone to pray that you will bless our own kingdom to the exclusion of all others. We see all that we do as good, excusing our political excesses by claiming that our wars were fought in your name. A piece of cloth with stripes and stars so easily becomes the banner of the Lord. Political systems working to our personal and tribal advantage appear to us as heaven blessed. Else why would they have succeeded? The tattered coat of the crucified Messiah can be defended with carnage, and now with one push of a button we can kill a hundred million human beings, all in the name of the gentle Galilean, silencing also the singing of birds and the bleating of lambs. God told us to do it. Onward Christian soldiers!

Things are bad enough as it is,

Jesus seemed to be praying. The gay colors of temptation lead us on. The things of this world are too much with us. So please, Father, don't make things worse. Don't you tempt us also. The temptations of Caesar and Mammon are sufficient.

Strange petition, this one. Lead us not into temptation. Why make such a request of the Infinite? Why would kinfolks lead their own kind astray?

Temptation? What kind of temptation? Is it some kind of test? Is it like a wife exposing her husband to harlotry to see if he is true to her? Does the Father drag us by the alluring campground of Satan and let the dazzle blur our vision?

Apparently so. For only Satan, to put it in at once primitive and modern terms, can tempt us. Temptation is synonymous with evil, or the potential for the doing of evil. One is not tempted to do the right. One is only tempted to do the wrong. Why would God, Dieu, Mungu, Big Daddy take us past that mudhole?

It is the blessed curse of freedom. In His own image, created He them. A little lower than the angels. Free as the birds. Free as God. Even Jesus seemed to shudder at the thought. "Don't do that to us, radical Father. Take it back. Don't give us such license. Don't tempt us with liberty because we're going to mess it up."

But the Father to whom he prayed *is* radical. Radical enough to create us free. Radical enough to create things that would tempt us, things we can appropriate for our own destruction. Radical enough to test us. Jealous. Even what we call mean.

Why did He do it that way? Why didn't he make us his happy puppets, laughing and dancing all day with Big Daddy pulling all the strings, lolling through life on some benign conveyor belt?

Mean enough to test us. Good enough to hear us when we are bold to say:

Lead us not into temptation.

But deliver us from evil

But wait. Abba is not so mean after all. He has the final say. Satan, Evil, the Devil is the enemy, and we are exposed to him, tempted by him, often deluded by his extraordinary wiles, charm, piety and goodness. He makes attractive offers and in our freedom we accept. But the final battle has already been won. Only we mortals are subject to the controlling influence of the Evil One. God is not.

More than once, the prayer of Jesus is an offer to abdicate, to yield the will, the freedom with which we are endowed back to the will and freedom of the endower. Yes, Thou hast given us a kingdom but we want *Thy* Kingdom to come. *Thy* will to be done over the free will Thou has given to us. Thou hast given us the earth and told us to have dominion over it, to subdue it and run it. Now we are asking that things be on earth the way they are in heaven. And yes, the humanistic unbeliever is right: it's a cop-out. We are asking for help, for rescue, redemption. We are asking for Grace, that something be done for us which we cannot do for ourselves. It is the total dependency of the child again. We are God's little cop-outs. And why not? God is God is God is God is God is God.

Deliver us from the Evil One. That is the ultimate petition. Never mind the temptations. We know they're out there and we know we'll strike at the baited lure of Satan and Caesar, become ensnarled in the pseudo-sophistication and false security of their offerings. Caesar and the Devil are powerful. But only second best.

We are asking God to be the grand exorcist, to deliver us surely and finally forever from the grasp of the Evil One, the one Scripture calls Satan. His seductive decoys bring us to certain treasons against the Kingdom of the Father unless the Father Himself rescues us from his rampant mischief. "Deliver us from the Evil One" is a much more serious matter than "Lead us not into temptation." With our own strength and resources we can resist temptations. But the power of sin and death, the brainchild of Satan, is too much for us. Perhaps no other passage of Scripture so succinctly demonstrates the love of Jesus. He taught us to ask the Father to deliver us from the

Evil One. And shortly thereafter he became the instrument of the deliverance through his execution and resurrection. The last enemy was conquered—death. The power of Satan is broken. We are delivered from the Evil One. Hallelujah!

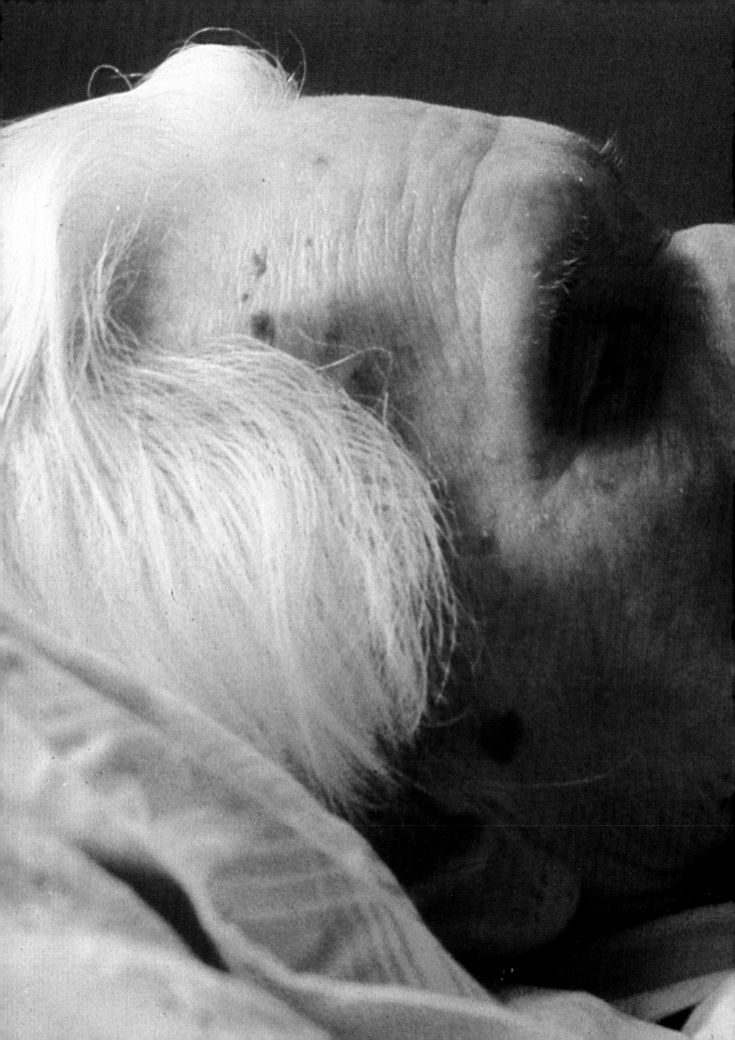

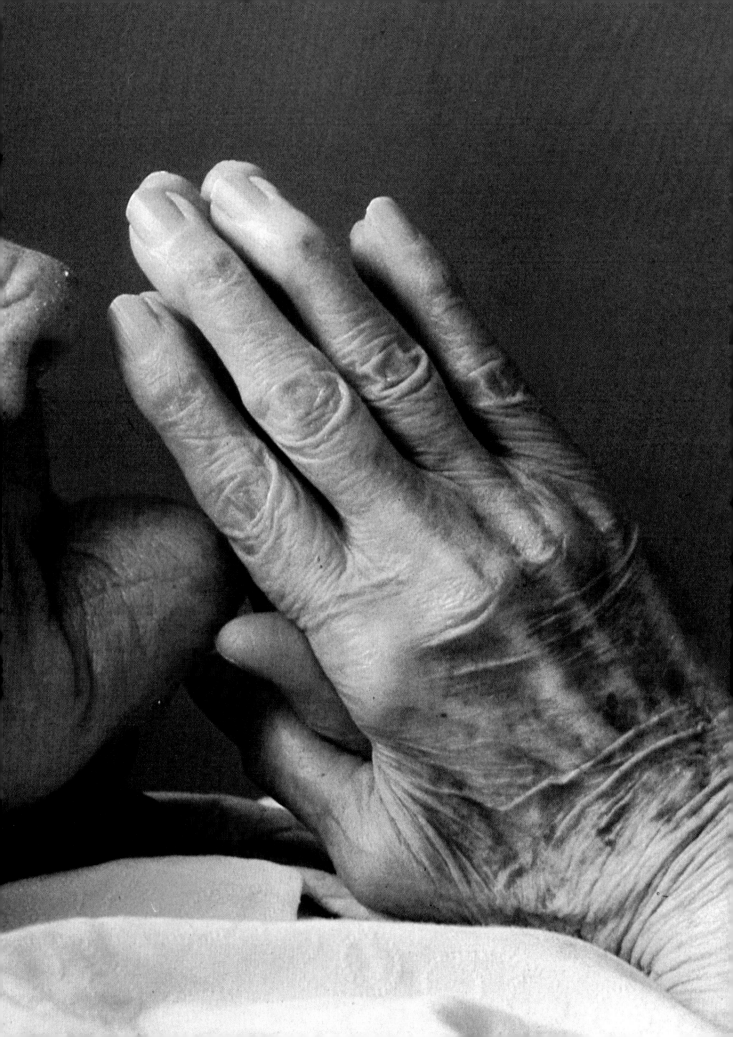

For thine is the kingdom

Whosoever shall not receive the kingdom of God as a little child, shall not enter therein.

A little child with a temper tantrum, kicking and screaming, holding her breath until she turns blue because she can't have her way?

A little child pushing all the others in the kindergarten to get the last cookie?

Ever watch a four-year-old spitting in his mother's face, yelling, "Shut up! I hate you!" Cute little fellow, eh? Those who talk of the innocence of a child have never been a parent, nor watched the spite, jealousy and self-centeredness of the young. Little sinners. That's what they are.

But how we love them! How Jesus loved them. "Let the little children come to me, for of such is the kingdom of heaven." It was the total dependency of little children of which Jesus spoke. They have no alternative. The little girl holding her breath, or the little boy spitting in his mother's face will die if the adult says, "Very well. If you hate me you don't need me, so I will leave you to your own mischief. Goodbye."

The baby lying so sweetly in subdued light is warmly covered, secure within the confines of the crib's slats, sucks with calm satisfaction on the pacifier and when he awakes will be changed and fed. He can do none of that on his own. It is not the first time he has relied upon the will and consideration of the big folks. He chose none of it. The act of procreation was performed without his consultation. The decision of the mother to carry him to deliverance was one over which he had no control. He survives only as their ward, a part of their kingdom.

And so do we. We enter the kingdom of the Father in total dependence or we enter it not at all. It is the kingdom of the Father. Jesus had prayed earlier that it may be on earth as in heaven. Now it is a simple affirmation and declaration: *"Thine is the kingdom."* We have no claim on it. We do not enter it by the bold good works of a grownup but by the dependency and naiveté of a baby. Our deeds do not enhance its power. The power is his also, Jesus is about to say. We do not enter it by our innocence because we are not innocent. We enter it as the child

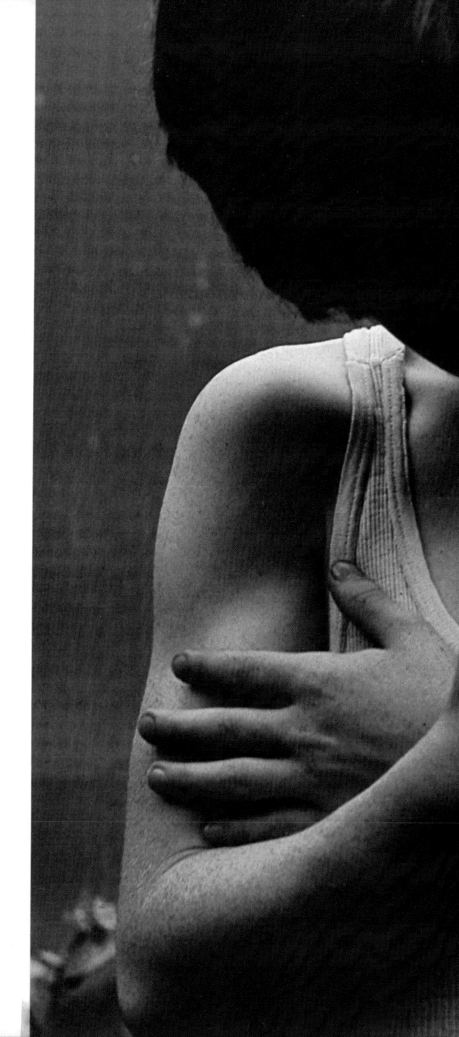

—helplessly dependent. God is God is God.

How do we respond to the kingdom which is His but in which we are free to abide? When we baptized our three-year-old son/grandson during Christmas breakfast he showed little interest in what we were about. When the ritual was finished, however, he asked what we had put on his head.

"Water," his grandfather replied.

"Why?" His grandfather talked to him of God, grace, forgiveness, even sin. As the homily continued he began to giggle, continuing to sop the runny egg yolk with the last of his biscuit. When he finished the little child was in the throes of a hearty belly laugh. Skipping from the table, returning to his world of play, he called over his shoulder:

"Well, well, Pappa. Thank you then."

Thine is the kingdom.

"Well, well. Thank you then." The only appropriate response. Our hope is in a kingdom already built. And owned.

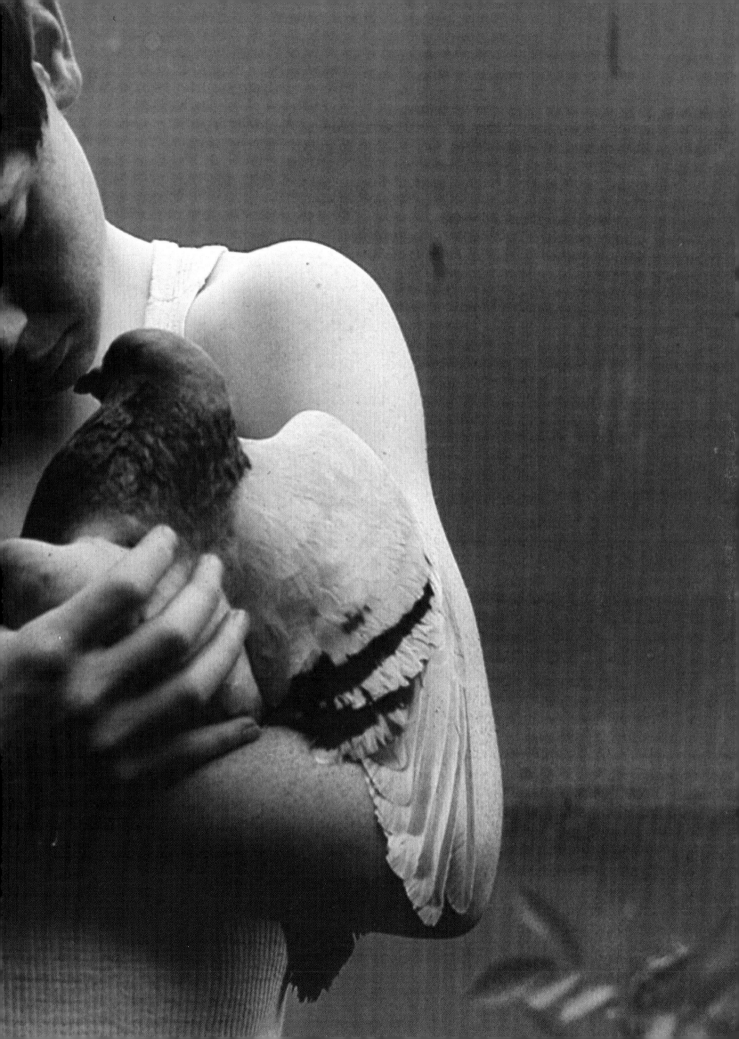

And the power

The whale oil in a flat clay lamp flickers dimly in the cave of a nomadic family, lighting the way for a mother and father to tend their newborn child. The power of light has overcome the power of darkness for them. Thine is the light.

Pieces of linen attached to a pole catch the wind and move a small vessel out from the shore of the Sea of Galilee. Twelve men, most of them skilled fishermen, listen to the words of the new friend they have chosen to follow. Later they marvel at the fickleness of the air. One hour they are gliding quietly across the smooth water and the next the turbulence is so great and the waves so furious they awaken their friend to save them. Peace. Be still. Thine is the power of the wind.

Water from a dammed-up timid stream is set loose on willing turbines and electricity is turned on two hundred miles away. Thine is the power of the water.

The people between the Tigris and Euphrates rivers designed round pieces of wood that would turn when moved along the ground. Their invention ushered in an era of wheelbarrows and Trident missiles. Whatever comfort and convenience the wheel might have brought, the mounting threat of a global holocaust bespeaks this as a time of folly and delusion. We saw it as an era of advancement and our continuing freedom may yet be exercised in wisdom. Whatever the case, we have it on the authority of Jesus that true power belongs to the Father and not to a world of gears and cogs. Thine is the power.

Lord Acton's words that "Power tends to corrupt; absolute power corrupts absolutely," might have been the greatest treatise ever on the sin of Adam and Eve in the Garden of Eden. Their quest was for power and because they sought that which was the holding of God they were rebuffed in the doing. Perhaps we are still committing the same simple and ancient sin, multiplied and magnified a trillionfold: Trying to become as God with the power of our own creation. The outcome is the same: Exclusion from the presence of God. Banishment to our own perdition.

Bishops, they say, have power. And presidents, premiers, senators, czars of commerce and lords of the Cosa Nostra. Thine is the power.

A little brown hen clucks and scratches outside our window, uncovering food for her week-old chicks, calling attention to it by her sounds. The little ones gather close and two of them fight over a small grub. She stops it with a warning squawk. It is starting to rain now. She takes cover under a shrub, spreads her wings slightly and the biddies scamper underneath her.

Thine is the power.

Mother to Child
(Joining the Resistance)

Your sleeping head baffles me;
my hands remember loving
the small shape of it
even though the head
is hardest to birth.

The mouth forgets it might
release angels
or welcome demons
and resigns itself to words,
eroding slowly,
but skin never forgets as it sags
how it sang.

The first time I held you,
your thin spine on my palms,
fragile as the curled grey spines
of shrimp,
my hands were happy all day.

I can't believe that soon
you will join the resistance
because it's better to die
quickly, in battle
than slowly of hunger.

The wind doesn't feel sorry for us.
We always mean to take root
but our feet recall
the happiness of dancing
and we come to realize that hunger
erases the past
as surely as greed.

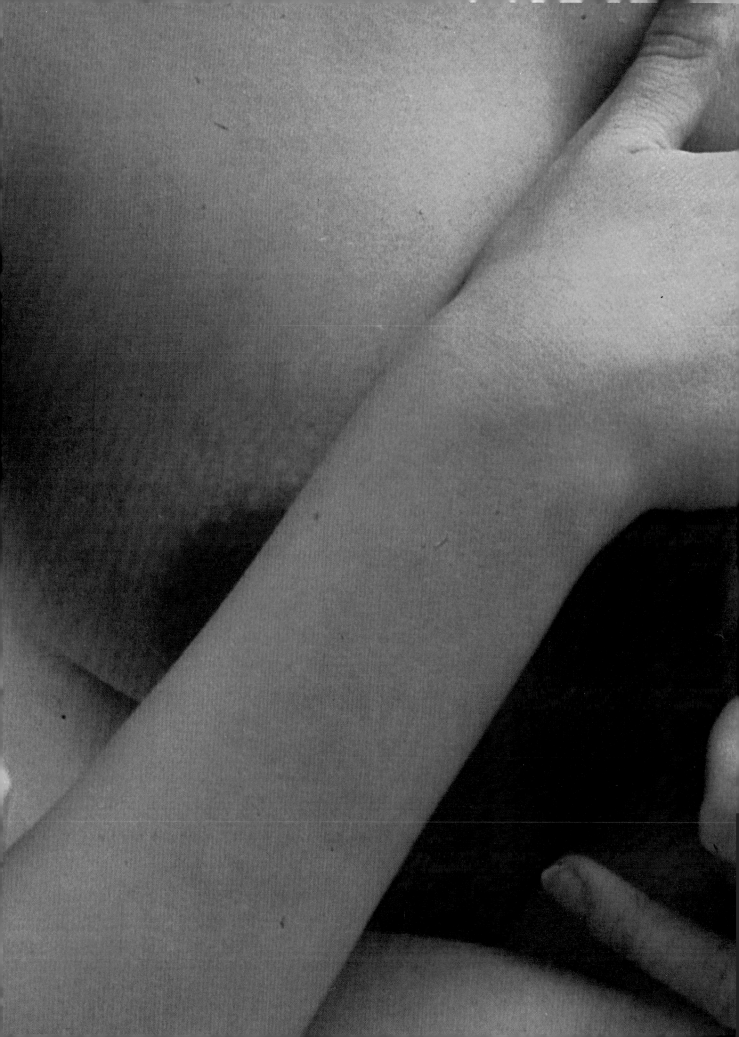

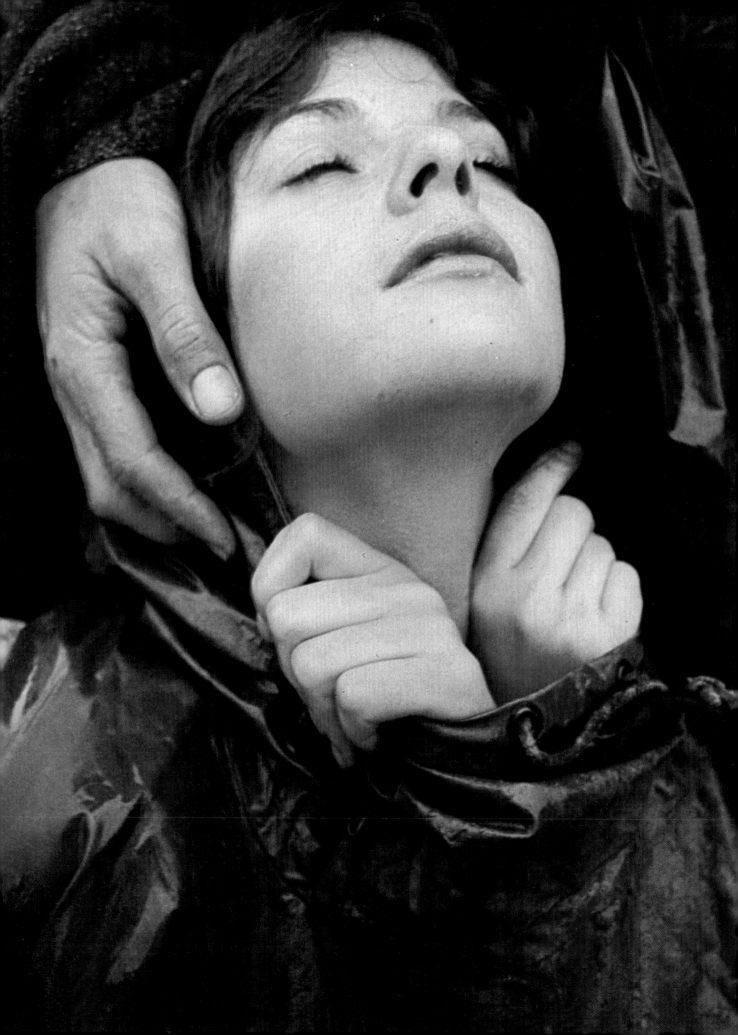

And the glory

Honor, praise, adoration credit belong to God. None to Satan. None to us. For Thine is the kingdom and the power, and the glory.

For means *because*. Because the kingdom, the power, the glory are yours, you can deliver us from the Evil One. That is th reason.

Majesty. Sovereignty. Splendor. Magnificence.

Words. Nothing but words we have made up. We apply them to someone we call God but none of them is applicable. And our spiritual ancestors were not always sure that the word G-O-D was appropriate. Yahweh was a name they used. But it was too sacred to pronounce so they substituted "adonai." So holy, mysterious, removed that it was said aloud but once a year and then by the highest of the priests. Who could know the name of the nameless One with enough certainty to recite it aloud. I AM THAT I AM hath sent you. And for a time that was the name for the nameless One: I will be present where I will be present. I will do what I will do.

Beyond language. Nameless One is nameless One is nameless One. Even then we have to reckon with some plural pronouns: "Let *us* create man in *our* image." They weren't even sure of the number. No wonder they had to make up a name. Did they also make up a gender? Who knows for sure. Mystery, the most authentic reality. God is God and then a period.

Just do baby chatter when you are searching for a name to address the—the what? Mystery. Just say, אבא. Big Daddy.

From a lonely roadside in Galilee to Nacogdoches, Texas.
Kinfolks.
Trust. The nonsense of trust.
What's your mamma's name, child?
Higher than eagles fly. Further than the compass points.
Kingdom without constables.
Though he slay me . . .
No petroleum? Ergo no missiles. On earth as in heaven.
Hostess twinkies? Bread.
No longer holding our misdeeds against us. Faults forgiven.
Freedom to go. Freedom to stay.
Steeples are pretty. Don't tempt us please.
The devil is after us. Save us from the macho bastard.
Kingdom.
Power.
Glory.

Chiropractor

His hands lace the vertebrae,
turn the body on its axis
releasing lightning. His fingers
reach deep in the muscle, sensing
its need to let go of spine,
demanding each nesting disc
to link against the urge
to lie down.
The pads of his hands
a cataplasm
drawing out needles,
understanding how muscles knot
and betray the face
so that skin forgets
its one job is to contain.
A body might refuse
to believe each planet spins
alone in the dark, disturbed
only by meteors
battering its crust,
the way one stands outside the skin
of another
trying to beat himself in.
You want to refuse the fists of words
and believe each sound connects
in trust
the way the tiny ear-bones
shake together.
You almost think he knows
the body, the spine that walks,
but it's thirst he knows—
the thirst rising from the body
asking a drink from the air.

Forever

Forever never begins. Forever never ends. Forever has no extremities. No end pieces. No middle or borders.

Forever is something like never. Never will not ever end because it will not ever begin. A million years is a thousand thousand portions of time. One day it began and one day it will end. A million years is the clock ticking, the peeling of pages from the calendar and happy new year again. Chronos. Time measured. It is a long, long time but within the realm of our comprehension. Long time passing but it does. Forever is not a long time because it is not time at all. Because it is not time it is beyond our comprehension. The human mind has not been able to fashion any such concept. We walk around it, speculate, put some words together. But when we finish we have said our words and nothing more.

"And God said unto Moses, I AM THAT I AM, and He said: Thus shalt thou say unto the children of Israel, I AM hath sent me unto you . . . this is my name forever." When some of Jesus' contemporaries argued and tried to trick him with logic of their own design he said, "Before Abraham was, I am." Not "I was in the past," nor "I will be in the future." I AM. Abraham was within the clock. His days were measured by the calendar. I AM. Forever. No end pieces.

Kingdoms of the earth rise and fall. Begin and end. Stubble taken by the whirlwind. David slept with his fathers. Solomon slept with his fathers. Jeroboam, Rehoboam, Abijam, Asa, Ahab, Churchill and Roosevelt, mighty rulers of the earth. All of them died and slept with their fathers and another reigned in their stead. Few of them reckoned with measured time, but their "never in a thousand years" had a brief echo and was gone. Short glory. Power. Glory. Gone. Gone. Gone.

For *Thine* is the power and *Thine* is the glory. Forever. So Jesus told us to pray about time not measured. Not passing. And not really time at all. Time is a word. Our word. The unword of God is I AM. The tense forever present. No past. No future. I AM THAT I AM.

Anglo-Saxons refer to I AM THAT I AM as God. Would Ole Blue, or Rambling Rose have been any more of a sacrilege? Is that why Jesus told his disciples just to call him Big Daddy (Abba) when they wanted to address him? (Sometimes there is a thin line between praise and blasphemy.)

Jesus said pray that time may be no-time, that the kingdom with no first and last will also be on earth, that the will of the Father might reign in our midst, that the earth will not be destroyed as heaven will not be destroyed.

And the petition, like all the others, is answered. Even if we persist in our madness, the kingdom will go on forever. Even with enough hardware of destruction to kill every living person ten times? So what? Big Daddy says. What if the lunacy goes on and we cause the planet to crumble into a thousand pieces, each one hurling through space devoid of gravity to pull them back together?

Forever.

What if we do the same with the moon where we have already planted our feet and banner? It is within our power (frailty) to bring the galaxy to a succession of collisions and orbital confusion. What then?

I AM THAT I AM has the power. And the glory.

Forever. And FOREVER.

Grace

". . . and the word was made flesh"

Was it when my son kicked out of me
that I began the slow crawl
out of myself?

Driving alone at night
I'm stunned at what metal
can do to metal,

pushing it back in on itself
like bodies
crashing into bodies
when they could easily
open
to take in,
to utter out.

Power

First thing you remember was you
* threw yourself*
at the foot of the stereo
where your father played Mendelssohn
and cried and cried until
you hoped he'd bring you
to the circle of his lap.
But he thought you slightly odd
for a boy of five.

Maybe your mother's face or the face
* of the music*
across your young breath
would have saved you
or will yet
from your father's deathly wait

that keeps him pinned
to the horizon.

The clear voice of your flute
urges you to love the air
which carries and kills
each sound only once—
the same air that keeps you here,
wears you down.

You wish for simple things
*   —a nap,*
a woman, a sandwich. There are
bigger, more terrible things
to wish for.

Talking

Words come out
one at a time,
find a target
or travel through air
so far
they are harmless.

But thoughts—like those maps
of constellations—
become whole lives,
nets,
like string figures kids weave
across hands.
The pianist, magically, moves
all fingers at once.

If I want to tell you this music
I have to begin
somewhere,
but then your *mind might map*
the Big Dipper,
might be impressed with another galaxy
altogether.

The mouth opens
and like Orion breaking apart,
spits one star at a time.

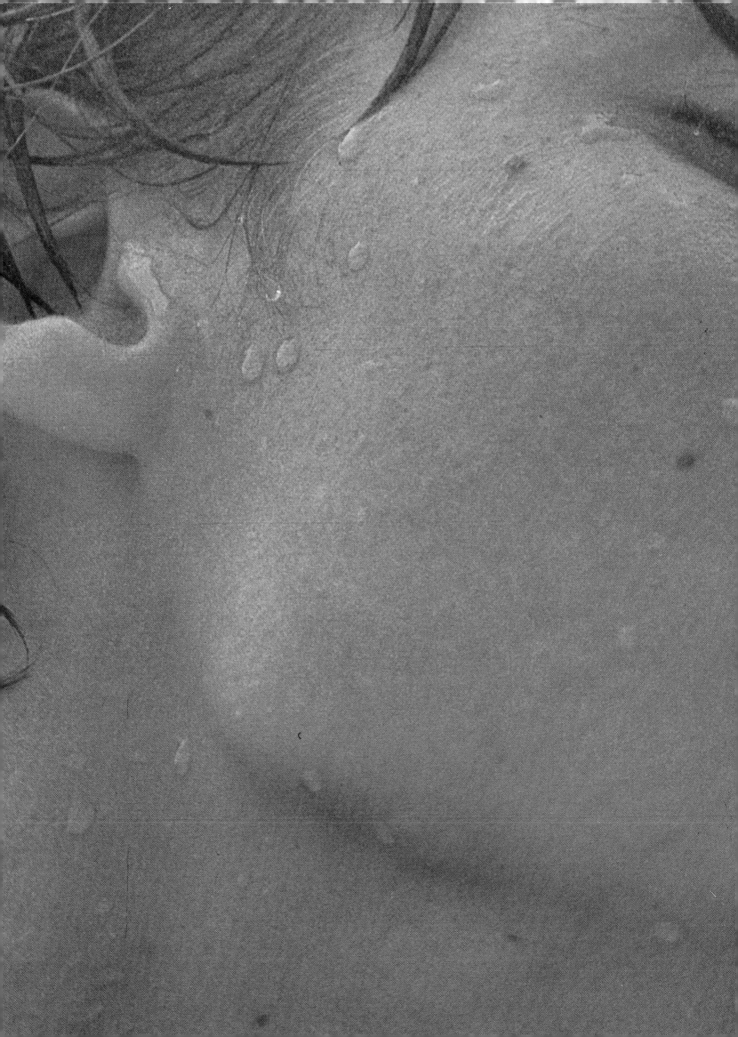

Amen

Never say amen until the prayer is over. AMEN. So be it. God is God is God is God is God. AMEN.